Healing Hullabaloo

Healing Hullabaloo

Edwin Bokert

To order additional copies of this book, contact:
Xlibris LLC
1-888-795-4274
www.Xlibris.com
Orders@Xlibris.com
546937

DEDICATION

I have thought and thought and am unable to enumerate the number of people who have helped me on my path as a writer and to whom I am endlessly grateful.

The first person is my wife who has given me more than anyone else in the world, in so many ways. not the least of which is to encourage whatever talents I possess. No one comes close to her in this respect.

The second individual is Sarah Taylor Izzo, without whose dedicated assistance I may never have completed this book of poetry.

These loving women are the two to whom I am most indebted.

CONTENTS

A Surprise 1
The Bliss Void 2
Names Of God 3
Rage 4
The Stupa At Boudha 5
I Had A Dream Last Night 6
'Tis Possible 7
Leaving Mexico 8
Whom Once I Loved 10
The Coin 11
I Sit To Meditate 12
The Benediction 14
Love's Smear 15
Love's Refuge 16
One Wish 17
Lord Of Life And Light 18
One With Wisdom 19
Basics 20
Lawn 21
Intake 22
For The Last Time 23
The Heroin Addict 24
Cape Dusk 25
Memory 26
After The Operation 27
Love Once Flourished 28
Stages In A Man's Life 29
I Know Not How 30
Who Are You? 31
The Pine Box 32
Eternity's Music 34

Vigil 35
My Search For Peace 36
Beatitude 37
Learning The Truth 38
Relationships 39
Bowery Visit 40
My Teacher 41
When No Rites Of Dawn Rise 42
They Wear Old Soiled Shirts 43
Sand 44
Fearful Ones 45
Two Truths 46
Namo Amida Buddha 47
Crows 48
The Settled And Unsettled Sleep 49
Gull Walking 50
Vet In Counseling 51
Once 52
The Oak Tree 53
A Tummy Ache 55
The Treadmill 56
A Dream Of A Monk 57
The Hill In Parphing 58
9/11 59
The Forest 60
A Soldier's Story 61
Pushing Eighty 62
Loss 63
Walking On 2nd Avenue 64
A Duality Thing 66
The Streets 67
The Pin 68
Letting Go 69
Voices In The Late Hours 70
Mantras 71
Our Eyes Shun 72
What More Could One Ask For 73
The Rabbi On The Subway Floor 74
How To Handle Pain 76

Morphing 77
Ascalepius... 78
Good Old Pop 80
Who Am I.. 81
Vet Vision 82
Praise To The Precious Teacher 83
The Love Addict... 86
Hey White Man 88
Foundations... 89
Headquarters 90
Healing 92
Reflections From Native Poetry 93
Now.. 94
My Birthday.. 95
Nirvana And Samskara.. 96
The Black Newman Moment.. 97
My Guru 98
My Frail Self 99
The Poltergeist 101
A Rose Is A Rose Is A Rose 102

A SURPRISE

Mysterious looking
Monastic like
Building below
We discovered it
As a dilapidated
Old monastery
Like an ancient
Manuscript placed against one
One of the hills
The door was wide
Open and we
Walked into
A desert storm of dust so thick
It is difficult
To breathe

Three monks
Are sitting
Beside the shrine
Their robes are dirt red
We sit crossed legged
Beside one of the two small open
Windows in the
Shrine room
Dwarfed by a
Statue of Guru Rinpoche
We are suddenly
Greeted by two small
Boys dangling
Their heads like puppets saying
In English
"Happy birthday"
"Happy birthday"

THE BLISS VOID

She wears her hair loose
Flowing down the back of her
Shining stream in which I dip my fingers
Greek proportioned body, soft, yielding

She lies down covering her hair
Her muscles relax, legs spread apart
To take me in like a windswept branch
In this Aeolian summer's drifting wind

Her mouth is half open as she
Anticipates the soft touch of my
Exploring tongue as she slides hers
Alongside until our tips touch

Our bodies ride in perfect rhythm
Our eyes gaze at each other
Everything moves but our glowing eyes
Then we explode into energy

What had been matter dissolves
into the insubstantial.
The bodies, the bed, the room,
All dissolve into
A bliss void.

Names Of God

Just joy
Eh ma ho
Mother of pearl moon
Secrets of the Baobob
Wheel of time
What doesn't come, stay, or go.
Clear empty sky
Cosmic comedy
Unseen wind.
Tide of coming and going
Sun lit snow
Not birth, not death
In infinitely adaptable water
Evening red
Spaces in the bramble bush
Dancer of dissolution
Not one nor the other
Ocean of space
Death which liberates
tan trickster
Kaleidoscope
TAOW
Horyu-ji: Temple of Exalted Law
Gateless gate
Eye of the hurricane
Deep silent sound
Lotus born
He ho, nobody home.

RAGE

I Rage Against This Rush Of Life
The Youthful Hopes
That Later Deepen In Despair
Deaths Dust That Chokes

I Cry My Angry Tears To God
For Transitory Things
Love Lost And Shining Beauty Dimmed
For Soon Broken Wings

For Shelters And Safe Places Built
Which Now In Ashes Lie
For Those Who Come Together And Must Part
Those Born, Who Die

I Turn My Back On Life And Death
These Masks Of Time
Who Conjure Up Empty Dramas Of Illusion
In Their Sequential Line

THE STUPA AT BOUDHA

We climb the terrace
To the graying dome
Look into the golden, orange setting sun
To see above the shadowed world
A last glowing glimpse
Of the luminous
Pink/white peaks
Of the Himalayan jewels
And for a moment
We who behold
And that which is beheld
Have no difference between them.

I Had A Dream Last Night

I had a dream last night
I was writing on a parchment
The attributes of his holiness
Dudjom Rinpoche, slayer of obstacles
The wisest men I had ever known
His mind was his jewel
Of pristine awareness
His mind had discernment
And was a mirror like, reflecting
All the worlds phenomena.
It was vast, permanent and pure
Forever benefiting others
I awoke and said out loud
Eh ma ho -how wonderful
What a blessing to have been
In his presence, receive teachings
From him. The world was
Blessed with his wisdom
And I dropped to my knees
Offering my heartfelt tears in gratitude

'Tis Possible

'tis possible
To leap into
Eternity
Insouciently
Abandon fear
Desire too
Jump deep

Plunge nonchalant
Not loose nor taut
Without support
Of hope or
Parachute
Of meaning

To crash without
Collision land
No where
In air
Not be nor
Nor not be
That's the ultimate.

LEAVING MEXICO

Christmas day we
Ferry to Hinit Zio
Debark and begin
To climb steep
Stairs cluttered
With a variety of shops

Brightly woven rugs
Hand painted bowls
Carved wooden figures
Of old men dancing
Wearing straw hats
Were being sold

Also a few
"Day of the Dead"
Figures were displayed,
A paper mache dandy
Stood out from
The others

His skull seemed
To be smirking
He leaned on a
Black cane with hubris

He wore a blue velvet jaunty jacket
Slim white trousers
And a black tilted
Top hat crowned
His air of obvious arrogance

The day of the dead
Seemed more colorful
Festive and alive
Than the hatless
Blue jeaned tourists of the living

We spent two
Weeks carefully
Exploring the
Shops while
Eating scrumptious tortillas
And downing beer

After lunch we
Huffed and puffed
Climbed a large hill to
A panorama of graves
Greeted us festooned
With flowering crosses
And colorful ornaments

Then like an Aztec
Sacrifice we
Felt our hearts
Had been cutout
As it was our
Day for departure

When we got home
And thought about our trip
We asked ourselves
Who are these people
Who could laugh at death?
Who are these people
Who could laugh
And make fun of death.

WHOM ONCE I LOVED

Whom once I loved, I cannot touch
Whom once I heard, is silent
Her eyes I gazed on gone from sight
Eyes that were sapphire and bright.

This love of mine I hoped to wed
So each of us could be fulfilled
Whence did she come and wither go
Her sad smile no longer glowed.

I feel I'm dying in my grief
Her food of love had given me life
Her sparkling soul slipped through my hand
Into the bleak smothering sand.

Her sounds gone like dying bird's cries
Echoes drifting through the dune's sighs
Off the coast now comes black stormy winds
Oh Father forgive me my sins!

THE COIN

Walking in a
Shrouded forest
I spy something
Shining behind
A cluster of ferns
I stop and
Pick it up
An ancient coin

On the one
Side it is
Dirtied and
Caked with mud
On the other
It is
Clean, shining
And golden

On its golden
Side it is just
Right, on its
Muddied side
It is just right
A precious
Ancient coin
Just as it is.

I Sit To Meditate

I sit to awaken the sleeping Buddha
I sit to see God, but not through a glass darkly
I sit to chant the ninety nine names of Allah; one after the other as in a rosary.
I sit to worship He who died and rose again
I sit to rejoice in the Lord of the dance
I sit as a corn kernel offered in the morning to the new day's Sun
I sit to honor Earth for her gifts which sustain all life
I sit as whispered prayer to the gentle Guadalupe
I sit to think of a question for the Rebbe and receive a dollar
I sit to be enthroned as Quetzalcoatl, the plumed serpent
I sit to become pristine awareness
I sit to became the precious teacher, Guru Rinpoche, who buried treasure everywhere even in my heart
I sit to wipe the dust from my mind's diamond
I sit to become black, white, red, and yellow
I sit to be a rainbow
I sit to watch whatever arises arise and whatever ceases cease
I sit to know the "I" and "sit" are words
I sit to sense the smile of Ghandi who said the name of Ram, in the garden, when he was shot
I sit as burning body in the ghat in Varanasi
I sit to breathe in suffering's carbon monoxide
I sit to breathe out the pure air of compassion
I sit to help you, only if you consent to be helped
I sit to help myself despite myself
I sit to find myself, not who you say I am nor who I say I am
I sit to lose myself, like writing my name in ink on water
I sit to find you after all these years
I sit to let you go and weep when you left and I am alone
I sit because it feels good
I sit because it doesn't feel good and I'm trying to make it feel good
I sit to feel delight in the first bite of a champagne truffle
I sit to see Race Point in a peach dawn

I sit to see the Sandia Crest in a mauve sunset
I sit to heal all beings, with my wings of swords and flames
I sit to be Nagarjuna,
King of the Nagas who, as he meditated was overheard to say,
"I do not sit, do not not sit, not both, not either."

THE BENEDICTION

Old Trinity Church
On Staten Island
Gave sermons,
Not helpful
Except when I
Slept through them.
But what did
Inspire me

Was the pastors benediction
"may you have
The peace
That passes all
Understanding."
That's it!
Not interested
In goodness, want peace.

Once heard
Tibetan monk
In red robe
Read from
A sacred text
"That beautitude
Is the repose of
All named things."

Yes! I got
To stop thinking
Meditate more.
Then I'll
Have peace
Like the feeling
I have just
After I
Get layed.

Love's Smear

Outside is Guston's smeary sky
Inside is my smothered sign
I breath in, then out
No balm no release
I smother my grief

The last great oak
Lost today all its float
It's leaves scattered on the ground
Night has now crept around
My tears are kept bound.

I open my mouth
A soundless oath
Ed Munch's foment
Silent its torment
this black Newman moment

I was poured in honeyed love
Held head high above
But lost sight
That it was now night
I smothered my fright

Long auburn hair
No longer there
Emerald almond eyes
Gone are these ties
She is a field lies

Van Gogh's crows come for me
I wait cravenly
Tremble patiently
Knowing love is the bloody smear
Where once was Van Gogh's ear.

LOVE'S REFUGE

Love's refuge but
A nomad's tent
Pitched in a barren land
A seeming shelter
Against the nights wind,
Uprooted in a gray dawn

A pale fire lit
In the mornings chill
Snuffed out in changing winds
Leaving its ashes
Scattered and buried
In the days shifting sands

Twilights embers light
Dusks new camp
Offering its illusion
of fading warmth
Before nights reality
Strips us naked and chilled.

ONE WISH

If you had one
Wish in your life
What would it be?
A million dollars?
Be brilliant like Einstein?
Paint like Rembrandt?
Live the life of Don Juan?
Have a life span of 100?
The Dalai Lama was asked
What his wish would be
He said: "I would wish
To be a wounded animal."

LORD OF LIFE AND LIGHT

Lord of life and Lord of light
Save us from our war filled plight
Gracious savior strong to save
All young dying soldiers brave

Ease their struggle pain and death
Love them in their dying breath
Guide them to your light of peace
Raise them up as each does cease

War takes their bodies as a thief
Their lives are snatched away so brief
They knew not day but only night
Bring them to your homes true light

We see young heroes brace
Stand by your recent grace
Recalling you had had your days
Knowing death could be your way

Lord of life and Lord of light
Show them all your golden sight
Hold them in your luminous hand
Bring them to your light filled land.

ONE WITH WISDOM

Wisdom is orange
Red gold and clear
Morning with no trace of fear

Past the long shadows
Of the dark night
Reflections of crystal
In the first light

Unified mandala
Suffused with sun
The morning and riser
Orange and one.

Basics

"how do I love thee
Let me count the ways
I love thee to the depth
And breadth and height
My soul can reach"
"I need a hug"

"A thing of beauty is
A joy forever, it's lovliness
Increases, it will never
Pass into nothingness
But will still keep a bower for us"
"I need a hug"

"Out of the night that covers me
Black as the pit from
Pole to pole. I thank what ever
Gods may be for
My unconquerable soul."
"I need a hug"

"It matters not how
Straight the gate how
Charged with punishment
The soul, I am the master
Of my fate. The captain of my soul."
"I need a hug"

Lawn

My dandelions roared
A pride of them
But I wasn't proud
It looked like a jungle
Desperate to be trimmed
But I'm not good at neatness
They grew into crab grass
They burnt into brown patches
My wife fired me
Hired a gardener
I'm not good out of doors

INTAKE

"My ma calls me nigger man
Ah jes' be shit to her
Done lets me play outside
If Ah complains she beats me
Ah gets ma assed kicked all-time

Dah man turns out da goddam lights
So Ah sits in de dark
Turns off da goddam phone
Coulden talk ta nobody
Nuttin' in da goddam rafrigareta
So Ah sits dere doin' nottin'
maybe tinks 'bout getting' high

Ah walks da streets 'bout 2 in da morning'
Be waitin' for somebody come up
'n try 'n rob or mug me
Ah wants somebody to do dis
Den ah could kill da mothafucka
But ah walks 'n walks 'n nevah sees nobody

One night Ah picks up dis rough trade
Ah takes 'em home 'n he gets me off
Ah goes inta ottter room ta roll a reefer
He sneeks up behind me
And hits me wit' a beer bottle
Blood starts droppin' all ova da rug
Ah gets a knife but he books

First time ah trys it when ah be 12
But nuttin' much happens ah jes get sick
Den ah tries it again when ah be 18
Dey calls an ambulince
'm rushes me at da hospitel
But someday ah's goin' do it by getting high
Jes get off 'nevah come back."

FOR THE LAST TIME

For the last time
I embrace her in my tears.
The melody of my love
Melds into the song of my sorrow
And a new voice is heard,
A compassionate loving grief.
How can my love hold such sadness?
How can my despair
Contain the comfort of joy?
Why must they be one?
It is unendurable.

THE HEROIN ADDICT

Told me
He has hidden redeeming worth
Sometimes mutters prayers
To the skag
For release

No interest
In quitting heroin
Getting a job
He is alive and dead
I, the therapist
Supposed to breathe life
Into him

Sometimes there is nothing
You can do
Except you talk
And watch them die.

CAPE DUSK

Foot imprinted dusk dunes,
Race Point relics
of sunbathers past
and evening's mottled ocean
left over
from lingering waves
of beach blanket
conversations.
September nights
are cool on the Cape.
I sit wrapped motionless
in sweater and blanket.
Without moving one inch,
I draw closer
to the floodtide fingers
of the encroaching ocean.
In this borderland
of fading, glowing light,
I become aware
of a giant Thunderbird,
hovering in the West,
A deep violet,
horizontal wing of cloud,
two feathery edges
spread on each side,
eclipsing the sun.
The rim of the sun's egg
then crowns at the bottom
of this dissolving bird
and slowly slips
into the receiving sea.
As its flame is swallowed
night is born,
and that which once was
is not the same.

Memory

After my examination
The doctor told me
I have good news for you
And bad news.
"Tell me the bad news
First" I requested
"The tests show
That you have
Alzheimer's Disease"
"Well then what
is the good news?"
"By the time
You get home
You will
Probably have
Forgotten what
I just told you."

AFTER THE OPERATION

The old puss finally
Came home from
The hospital, her belly
Stitched, her pure
Silken skin is now
More like burlap
I try to caress her
Coarse canvas, searching
For some sensuality
But no; the pretty
Kitty is a tweed rug
A bit lumpy, I attempt a
Nocturnal exloration.
It doesn't help. I
Keep trying devotedly
Love however is
More mental now
When I keep exploring
Long enough I
Can feel warmth emerge
Under my arthritic
Carpal tunneled fingers

LOVE ONCE FLOURISHED

Love once flourished
Now lays pulverized
Like crushed rock

What I tried to build
Has this day fallen,
Broken beyond repair

Tenderly holding hands
Which radiated kind beauty
Once held loves meaning

Now a charnel ground.
I sit in loneliness
Impoverished of hope

A moonscape of despair
Merciless in its pain
With no solution

What is left now?
But to sit in this cemetery
And feel our separation.

STAGES IN A MAN'S LIFE

In the strong growing flowering years
With female teens in short, above knees skirts
Without any real hubris, I did consider
Myself, the Washington Monument

Then, as I reached pre-crumbling years
This proud, ever ready spelunker
Admitted needing help from a small, blue pill
I was the Leaning Tower of Pisa

Then entering the pyrite years
This proud and arrogant adventurer
Time of memories
I am now the Lingam memorial.

I Know Not How

I know not how
In the late night
Before dawn wakes

Out of the meeting
Of ground
And quiet sky

Before sun rises
There is a moment
Changing night to day.

WHO ARE YOU?

A politician who has lost most of his hot air
But is still flapping his lips

A 3 ring circus continuing to perform
After the tent has collapsed

Terminally ill man
Not yet ready for the final exhalation

An old fool barely able to walk, with
A glint in his eye

An insomniac rooster crowing before dawn

A night club monologist still doing his routine
After the audience has left

An experienced counselor who was long since
Forgotten all his training

A chronic guru to his wife who sits mute
With a knowing smile

A dutiful, responsible, unrepentant playboy

A fellow falling off a cliff
Complaining his shoes are too tight

A guy who feels like this and his
Teacher tells him you are that
And worse.

THE PINE BOX

Soon I'll be pushin' eighty.
This ain't no matter of glee
Soon I'll be pushin' daisies
Never got to my BO Tree.
Death should mean ceremonies,
But for me no choir, just cds.

At last I'm in this pine box.
Can't eat no bagels and lox.
This box is one empty place,
But at least it's full of peace.
No ceremonies at church
I feel sorta left in the lurch
But in box no phones, emails,
Nobody succeeds or fails,
No work I have to have done,
Just lay back, wiggle a bone,
No exploding bombs, rockets,
Eyes without their sockets.

Contemplating in coffin have
Nothing at all left to fear.
Hark! What's these musical strains?
Seeping through the wooden frames?
B Minor mass of old J.S. Bach
Faures' Requiem, all grand pax

I lay back, have sweet recall
Of the solemn funeral hall
I looked good at the viewing
Pink cheeks after some rouging
Alive I was mostly pale
Skinny bent over and frail.

At viewing a blue pressed suit
White shirt, red tie, looked real cute
Had black bags under eyes
Powder on face was a disguise.
That day I looked healthier dead
Then when I was supposedly alive.
Worries, frustrations, fears
Down here you're all in the clear
Ain't no more King Arthritis
Limping on streets to Godivas.
Death does make us all equal.

At present listen to Brahms
Not above my operatic charms
With half the audience coughing
Old gents opera nodding
Problem with pine box, one hex
Down here there's just no more sex.

ETERNITY'S MUSIC

My pine box suite is ready?
Got no nerves, I'm steady
Once in the box, quiet
No African riots
No bombs, wars, death
In box, nothing uncouth
No fears, worries, anger
Just contentment, languor
No emails, Iphones
No ring of old telephones
Here in box
Many requiems: Brahms
This can do no harm
Faure requiem, superb
This will not disturb
Even Dvorak, a delight
In coffin dwellers long night
Bachs B Minor Mass
Verdi's Dies Irem
All of us cheer 'em
Mozart requiem mass
The music and death, both last
What more could you want
An eternity studying Kant?

VIGIL

At dusk I walk
Slowly through the dark trees
And wonder at a voice
I hear among the branches

It trails through leaves
Like vapors from some unknown source
Streaking the sky with whispers
Unable to be comprehended

I yearn to hear the words
But night muffles me
Dampening my ears to the sound
Of this voice of dusk

Now in the hours of night darkness
I still wait the murmur
From the leaves and vapors
But the night has gone.

My Search For Peace

I read books
On the subject,
Consulted teachers,
Talked with friends,
Meditated on it.
All my stress
Filled, twitchy
Life I have
Yearned for peace.

The pastor of
Old Trinity Church
On Staten Island
Gave sermons,
Not helpful
Except when I
Gossiped through them.
But what did
Inspire me

Was his benediction
"may you have
The peace
That passes all
Understanding."
That's it!
Not interested
In goodness,
Want peace.

BEATITUDE

Once heard
Tibetan monk
In red robe
Read from
A sacred text
"That beatitude
Is the repose of
All named things."

Yes! I got
To stop thinking,
Meditate more,
Then I'll
Have peace
Like the feeling
I have just
After I
Get layed.

LEARNING THE TRUTH

Don't give me no grief
No theories, no beliefs
Your award winning poems
Your talked about tomes

You see, what I'm looking for
Is the truth, no less, no more
The truth is something you feel
An experience with which you deal

Put down Keats and Shelly
Truth lies lower in the belly
Cultures, traditions are all a pox
Truth lies more in a bagel and lox.

RELATIONSHIPS

Chogyam Trungpa
An old Tibetan Lama
From Colorado said
If two people get
Married there is
Always a problem

To me it seems like
The shore at Ocean Grove
The sea and
Sand are different
One is wet and the other is dry

This sea wets the sand and
The sand dries the sea
It is the marriage of
A wet sand or a dry sea
A relationship is soggy
Just like this.

Bowery Visit

I stand on line
Ladeling soup
In a Bowery hotel,
To lice infested
Tuberculotic,
Pneumonia ridden
Jobless, homeless
Men, my
Social work
Colleagues call them
Bowery Bums.

They line up
Waiting for
A sandwich or soup
Served by a
Bowery kitchen
Then go to sidewalk

To suck Thunderbird
"Biggest bang
For a buck"
They don't drink
So much as suck the
Bottles nipples
Like a breast

My Teacher

We have just finished dinner
The six of us: the venerable
Ontul Rinpoche, his sturdy
Young son and Sue and Orest
Whose home we were in
And my kindly wife and I

The monks want to take
A few photographs so
We move to the soft sofa
Rinpoche sits in the middle
Of my wife and I. He places
His arm around my shoulder

The joining of lotus lake lamas
And students now in New Jersey
Meeting like one family
Warm bean soup glows in our belly
And we have soft conversation
The monks want a photo of me.

My Guru and I hold
Hands and lean
Against one another
We are like a
Father and his son
Both of us are smiling

WHEN NO RITES OF DAWN RISE

When no rites of dawn rise
To inform the unlit ground
When night is tunneled
And signless
When procession of winds
Blow in unformed lines
Then all ceremonies of known things
No longer signify

They Wear
Old Soiled Shirts

They wear old
Soiled shirts
Patched,
Torn jeans.
Buddha books
Say that
Underneath
All that disgusting
Sickness they
Are all capable of becoming Buddhas.

I read the
Dharma books,
Get inspired
With compassion,
But when I
See these men
In their hotels
Smelling of
Vomit, urine, feces
I'm fearful
Of getting TB
Or lice jumping on me from them,

I must care for and
Develop homeless Buddhas
Tubercular Buddhas
Lice infested Buddhas
To help I must dig deep
Into my own compassion

SAND

The days taste is sand
Blowing into my mouth
Thinking of she
Who has gone
Where is the sweetness
No over ever
Promised me?

I think of her home
The lions claw
Oak table, with
High backed
Matching chairs
I imagine her
Exquisite Persian rugs

Recall the Himalayan
Peaks orange in the sunset,
Votive candles lit around the stupas
These scenes are now only postcards.
The beauteous sights gone forever
And all love will be gone forever
Nothing to hold and be held by.

Except this gritty air
God is the grit, our God of
Sand. I bow to his choking.
God mash your grapes
Into sweet nectar
Or shut my mouth
With dust forever.

FEARFUL ONES

Fearful ones
Who recoil at
The rising sun
During the day
Try to fly
but feel their wings
Are broken

When the black
Shroud of night
Is pulled over
Them, they live
Their nights in fear
And pray for the
Dawn of a new day

Know that
Wherever you
Go or stay or
On your journeys
A rich light
Forever luminous
Is always there.

Two Truths

Placed today in ground
Flowers purple brushed
Under a constant sky

An earthen mound
Its clay repository
Heaped in the open

Inscribed in stone
Soon weathered words
Content of space

Prayers quietly intoned
Disappearing in wind
Within silence.

Namo Amida Buddha

Lord of limitless light and life, Amida Buddha
I honor, praise and give thanks to you
For your great vow and compassion
I entrust my life and death to you
I come just as I am, Like Shinran
"A sinful mediocracy", a constant breaker
Of vows, of sexual misconduct and angry thoughts
But through your great vow and compassion
You save me and take me to your pure land
Just as I am, the good along with the bad
Your great compassion includes everyone,
Even the worst of sinners
This occurs not through my self power
But through your other power, saving me
At this very moment of my life and at the
Moment of my death, Namo Amida Butsu

CROWS

A few years ago
There were blue jays
Now crows have come

Hunched on branches
Cawing from the trees
Between the houses
Waiting for the drum

A red glare hangs
Over the town
And at the drum's beat
Crows fly to the arm
of the shaman

Each dawn he calls
To the high hill
Behind the houses
To the water
Which runs through lots
At twilight he calls to the crows
To cover the reddening sky
With their dark wings.

The Settled And Unsettled Sleep

In this quiet night
Torrents from the day
Ebb slowly
From the shores of memory

But beads of thought
Sink rapidly
In the sweet vapor
Of the minds settling

Yet in this stillness
Rising in thunder
Are the memories
Which remain unsettled.

Gull Walking

Grey, plump gull
On spindley legs
Fat bird on stilts
Wobbling briskly
Across multi shelled
Sand, where are
You going bird brain?

Not riding lapis
Waves
Or looking
For crumbs like
Others? You walk
In straight line
As with a purpose

But given no sign
Going some where?
Why force these
Questions on him
Gull, why am
I so bothered?
I should shut
My mouth and
Spread my wings

VET IN COUNSELING

At night this Vet
Recalled to me:
"It was cold in Viet Nam
A foliage refrigerator"

His breath stopped, no
Release, no relief,
Tries to blot out
Memories, can't do it.

Talked to buddies
"we get relief. someone
Gets shot
Death is biggest release."

"I see a body, we don't talk
Mute is best
Look at hole in
His head bloodied"

The action was
Exciting,
Gun shots sounded
Like type writers

ONCE

Once I ran hard
To catch fly balls hit
By opposing batters
Now I sit quietly
Benched by age
Once I cherished victories
Felt defeats slap
Now I watch robins
Across my lawn hop
I have no regrets
Life is running
It is also sitting
Lives in defeat
Inhabits victory
I am grateful
Lying in the casket
I will have all
My athletic medals on
I won't know it
Mourners above grave
won't see them
But many will have
Memories which did not die.

The Oak Tree

In our backyard
An oak tree stood.
Lean and bent,
Knotted and knarled
In grey wrinkled skin,
Its canopy once full, now cratered thin,
From autumn winds
Whispering through
Its dry leaves.

With trucks, sharp saws and ropes
Summoned were landscapers
"Amputate they growled
Two of its branches
Keep alive its chances"
One night the burden
Of a snowfall fell,
We feared the frail oak
Might be stricken down,
A large dead arm
Upon our home.
Our trusted tree
No more a refuge safe.

Again the tree men came.
With brute advice:
"It must come down
Become a stump."
I turned and threw
My arms around its trunk,
Felt alone and sad
For this worn thing

I heard a sigh,
It could have been the wind.
I sensed a beat,
It probably was my heart.
I threw my arms
Around its trunk
And whispered prayers
For all withered things.

A TUMMY ACHE

"A knowledge more than
Human possessed me. I felt
I was suddenly released from
My body and as pure spirit
Partook of a lovliness
I had never conceived."

So wrote Somerset Maugham
Of Larry Darvell of
His experience in the
Book "The Razors Edge"
When I was eight I was
Standing in my sun porch

Suddenly my body, the
Sofa, the floor, ceiling
Walls, rug, all material objects
were decomposed
The substantial dissolved
Into the insubstantial.

I was part of everything
And everything was part
Of me. All is one but
I received no joy but
I got a tummy ache
So hid under my covers.

THE TREADMILL

In my physical exam Doctor Serious asks:
"Why God build you? Make you for walking,
Not sit motionless on your old tush
Should jog in the park, watch birds and girls.

If you sit read, write, watch TV: Dead
Tests say your boat got no float
You look like Auschwitz man just make it."
I counter, "kings all comfy on thrones"

"Thrones, churches, health food shops not help you
Only this treadmill will save your tush"
With pride I say: "I meditate, chant"
He says: "oi vey snorts, dribbles, says "Dead"!

Tall, bony, Dr. Ichabod Serious,
Papist, hier-arch monologist.
"Treadmill or door" he says ex-cathedra
I make appointment following day

In gray walls, gray machines one pink nurse,
I come for my survival training.
Have on new red white and blue sneakers
Wear tennis shorts over knobby knees

I tried to make it upstairs to
The gymnasium, huffing and puffing.
Doctor looks at my lack of any
Muscles and he murmurs "Oy vey—a job we got"

A Dream Of A Monk

Last night I had a dream
I was in a large monastery
But bizarrely I was Ju
Mipan Rinpoche, a Tibetan
Monk I knew nothing about
Nor heard about him
Never read any of his books

I had a lighted torch
In my hand and here
And there lit the crown wicks of
Several clay
Buddha shaped figures
As if enlightening them

I awoke wondering who the
Hell Mipan was
I went to Google and was told the following:
There are two modes of valid cognition

"A conventional cognition
Of confined perception
And a pure vision"
My dream was the pure vision.

The Hill In Parphing

In monastic gloom we
See what has
Spontaneously
Arisen
Buddhas from
Clay mounds
A host of holinesses
Two cans of beans and
a can of Crisco
Were nestled alongside
The sacred figures

Meditating on the
Scene, a deep blue
Sparkling diamond
Light flashes
And became
Brighter than the Sun

In the monastery are
Two open windows
Two boys appear
Shouting "Happy Birthday!"
"Happy Birthday!"

9/11

We went to our churches and temples
Bag pipes played, incense raged, hymns were sung
All creeds filled places of worship from
"California to New York Island"

Volunteers gave blood, wrote checks, Counseled on that day
our entire nation mourned
On that day we became the living truth
Our forefathers had taught us. We are one
Nation under God. Indivisible.

THE FOREST

Ten white birch trees in a clump
Thin branches reach from their trunks
Clusters of leaves all move together
In this blue blustery sweeping weather
Like some unseen hand had them shaking
Ten slender trees a minion making

When the wind then increased its force
And the different leaves in the forest toss
The oaks, the cedars, maples, birches move
A varied, light and dark green grove
In this forest, nothing is contrived
Nothing needed from men to survive

At the picnic you think you are still
Not so, your lungs empty and refill
Red blood cells move throughout your body
Your precious lung, a force embodies
Inside and out there is this swaying
All nature is divining and praying.

A Soldier's Story

Buds fall down
Some read Bible
Others pray
Still no relief.

Corpses can't find God
Corpse leg is missing
We can't find it

Most soldiers pray
But say no response
We take communion
Still die

Kneel on knees, pray
Drink juice, eat bread
We know death well
But don't know God

PUSHING EIGHTY

No longer have
Ordinary thoughts
That's all
Circus mundis
Pre death bullshit
Death not monotonous
Angels chorus piped in
Light and earth fissures
Brahms, Faures
Requiems
No coughs
From audience
in coffins
Undistractabulus
Perenialus
I see saints deities
Wait for big boys
Lapis light glow
He will take me to
His blue paradise
Bro, you don't believe it
When you bite dust
You're scared shitless
For me
Hosanna in excelsius.

LOSS

Wings of filming
Curtains flare from
The open windows draft
For in my mind
Thoughts keep blowing
In a ceaseless breeze

I lie
in a fetal pose
Ask Myself how much longer
An iron weight presses down
On my chest
Fatigue pulls tight
Across my shoulder

Night drags on
Then slowly it
Begins to pale
Fingers of light
Touch my face
But the tips of
Light are still
Without solace
Memories of her
Have not gone
Not gone is endless

Questions arise
About continuing
Excoriated
I am unknown
Not human not
An animal
nor am I the dawn

WALKING ON 2ND AVENUE

I am walking
Up 2nd Ave
Passed a men's shop
With various sports coats

In the window
One catches my eye
Suddenly a salesman
Rushes out of the store

His first finger
He sticks in the
Lapel of my sports coat
I try to break loose

But his finger
Is like a metal
Hook I can't
Dislodge it

I cry out
"I'm just window shopping"
But he says "inside
You see better"

He drags me
By his strong finger
Into the store
"You see the quality?"

The sports coats
Are too gaudy
For my taste
Finally I cry out

"I'm just window
shopping", he argues
"These prices you can't beat
On Delancy Street"

Against my will
His finger still
Stuck in my lapel
He forces me

To see his collection
They are much too
Gaudy for me
I tell him

"I just like
This plain one"
He takes his
Finger from my lapel

Immediately I run
Out of this store
For one block
He chased after me.

Still holding the
Jacket in his hand
That I had
Originally liked

"He says for my kind
It's the best buy
On all Delancy Street."

A Duality Thing

My lama done told me
When I was in re treat, son
Your mind is a 2 faced
Duality thing
That leads you to sing
The blues in the night.

THE STREETS

He narrated to me in therapy
"the guys dat are woikin' get laid off
Fight wit' der wives, don' bodder wit'der kids
Drink a lot, get disgusted and book (leave)

Den der dese crazies walkin' round, doped up
On tranks from da state 'bins, dey live in
Roomin' houses, walk up and down all night
Sometimes go to liberies look at pitchers in magazines

Bout sundown da hookers start to
Walk da streets, da cars wit da
Johns cruise around. Fur 20 bucks
Ya could get blowed or laid, some
Goils wear knives in der stockings
In case dey pick up a weirdo

Da churches are filled wit ole
Women, sing hymns, sneak booze
Take sleepin' pills, believe in
Jesus, don' trust da streets
'Fraid kids will mug em
Dey could get mugged for a few bucks.

One client says you Tink
You're thurpy is gonna cure all dis?
Got a message for you
I plan to go sideways (suicide)
Dats my relief

THE PIN

I dreamt I looked
Down
And saw a
small slender elegant
Completely significant
Pin with a head on it
It was the most delicate
Exquisite object I had
Seen in a mellinium of decades or
Lifetimes ago
And to come across
This again in this
Vast world was
Unbelievable
I never thought
That I would ever
Find this again
A magnificent object
It was one of
The most felicitous
Ever made
And I had
Rediscovered it
It held the greatest
Significance for me
Beyond my ordinary
Comprehension.

LETTING GO

First a big hug
Then the tender
Touch of a kiss

I can't let you go
I won't.
When you're present

Or when you are absent
I see you everywhere
In my perception

In my mind's eye
Your brown
Flowing hair

Your Goddess shape
Tall regal, slender body
Your bright brown eyes

To clasp your hand
Is to hold
The entire universe

In one loving
Embrace I can't
Let you go, I won't.

Voices In The Late Hours

When voices in the late hours
And the thought sea calms
Like a lake on a windless night
My prayers ascend
Like the rising of vapors
And I am lifted to a place
Still as stone and crypt quiet
Where I have hope.

Mantras

Wet brown leaves
On the rain-stained sidewalk
Where I walk
A dirt grey sky lies
Behind trees half bared
Their black branches hanging down
Like limbs charred.

But I slowly walk
These early silent streets
And hear the calm call
Of a wren and listen
To the fine rains soft drone
On the wet leaves.

OUR EYES SHUN

Our eyes shun
What we seek
Removing us
From the glimpse
And threat of
Radiance
Protecting us
In the comfort
Of our blindness
The security
Of our suffering.

What More Could One Ask For

What is the peace
That passes all understanding
Mozart's horn Concerto, his
Requiem, Brahm's Requiem
Bach's 2nd Brandenberg Concerto
Dvorak's 8th Symphony
Beethoven's 9th Symphony

Then there is silence
No talking, no reading
No conversations
Not one thought
That was my whole day
Peaceful, it was heavenly

I nibbled a chocolate bar
Sipped green tea
Held hands with
My sweet wife
What more could
One ask for
From such a day.

THE RABBI ON THE SUBWAY FLOOR

In a subway
An aged Rabbi
Trips and falls
Questions God
"A tzim tzum?"

But on the
A train?"
God perhaps
Stirs slightly.
The Rabbi

Lands on a
Lady's soft lap,
Then to
The hard floor.
A failed Chagal

In exile
On the floor,
Embarrassed,
He argues
"God, I'm not

One of your
Broken vessels."
The Rabbi starts
To fan sparks
In his heart.

He cries out
"God, I'm fanning."
He wants a sign.
"Hey foyler, (Lazy ones)
I'm telling your ear

I want you
Should give me
A quick Tikkun" (a fix)
Over a loudspeaker
God thunders

"Where were you
When I laid
The foundation
Of the subway?
Who has put

Wisdom not kvetching
In the inner part?
Go and gird up
Thy loins
Like a man."

The Rabbi pulls
Himself to a seat
Softly begins to sing,
"Tumbala tumbala
Tumbala laika."

How To Handle Pain

Lying down
Helps relieve
The pain in hip

In bed
With heating pad
Is better

Best of all is
Wife massage hip
I massage her breast.

Morphing

I love a woman
To the depth and
Heights of my being
I can feel the love in all fibers of my body
There was no thing
In the world
That I loved more

I burst into tears
Unexpectedly
Suddenly, she left
Explosively
And I cried
And cried
For I don't
Know how long

But then I gradually
Morphed myself
Into a peace
A serenity
Sublimely
In this hour

The peace began
To ease and
I felt a profound
Sense of freedom
It lost all its
Limits and it
Became a freedom
Which was boundless

ASCALEPIUS

Ascalepius Roman
Shieskopf diety
You and your baths
Rituals, ceremonies
Devoted followers

I pray grant me
Dominus delectus
Snoozum, snozzorum
For what do I get
Wide awake
Beta waves. Thou
Milkless sleep
Depriving mother

Feckless father
Beer drinking foyler
I'm writing
To tell you
I no longer
Need you either
I found a
More potent parent
Benzodiazapine.

I sleep now
Seven to eight hours
Guaranteed
States three and four
Now a nice
Uninterrupted sleep cycle

But I must confess
A few side affects
Some mornings
I wobble a little
I forget things
All inconsequential
Compared with
My sleepus
Uninterruptus.

So fuck you
Ascalepius
And go
Play with
Your young boys.

GOOD OLD POP

"I wakes up in
Some god dam room
hemorraghing, stumbling
I'm fuckin' dyin'
Phoned old pops
He says"
You sound bad
Gives me
crisis number to call
He's busy today
Will phone tomorrow
I throw phone down
Then pick it up
Call crisis unit
Say Fuck you Pops
And pass out

Who Am I

I asked my Mother,
Who am I?
She replied,
My breasts gave milk.
I asked my Father
Who am I?
He said:
The harvest will come.
I asked a child
Who am I?
She said
Hippity hop
I asked a priest
Who am I?
He answered
"Consider the lillies."
I asked life
Who am I?
And a strong wind blew
Across the sky
And it was nameless.

Vet Vision

Lord of life and Lord of light
Save these soldiers from their plight
With your streaming lights please save
The dying soldier who fought so brave.

Ease their struggle, pain and death
Love them in their dying breath
Guide them to your light of peace
Raise them up as each does cease

Soldiers young without full life
Taken from the world so brief
Knew not the sun only night
Bring them to their homes true light

We send them all our deepest love
To their graves we stand above
We'll recall you all our days
Gifting you our prayers and praise

You will rest in pure lands light
Winged away from earth's dark blight
My arm will hold each ones hand
And there create a light filled band.

Praise To The Precious Teacher

When he taught.
The roar of his voice
Fell like the waters of Niagra
Over the students
Who sat in a awe
Of this unceasing flow.
All praise
To the Teacher's roar.
When he spoke
A bubble of joy
Arose in his voice
That would carry you
On a stream beyond words.
All praise
To the Teachers's joy.
During interviews
He would say,
You are struggling
To climb all the stairs
In the Empire State Building,
When the first step
Is no different
Than the last.
Then sometimes
He would hold a mirror
To your face
And you would see nothing
But the lined features
Of your own reflection.
All praise
To the Teacher's mirror

Let us offer praise
To the Precious Teacher
And all the teachers
Who are precious
the sun which warms
And lights our way,
And all its rays like fingers
Reaching to the corners
Of our cities and villages
And into the land of snows
With its hidden treasures
And visible sorrows.
Let us praise him
As we count to 12
The syllables
That circle unceasing,
Praise him, too,
As we count to seven
The lines of the prayer
The sky dancers taught.
3 words will also praise him
If they hit the essential target

Let us join hands,
We who gather in his name,
And chant our praise
To the precious Teacher,
Who is the Great Perfection
Of our own awareness,
The diamond's sparkle,
The foundation stone
Of the house we live in
The infinite reach
Of the cloudless sky
The sparking amethyst
In the crude geode,
The reflecting rainbow
Of the sunlit prism,
The simple love

Of one of us for another.
Praise to Guru Rimpoche,
The pristine energy
Of the full void,
Which is the body of truth,
The 5 families
And their rapturous wisdoms,
Which is his body of bliss,
And his earthy body
Which coaxes us
To jump into his lap
That he might hold
And teach us.

THE LOVE ADDICT

I feel a deep melancholy
Seeing her beautiful
Face and body as in
A vision, as in a dream
I can not shake my sadness

She is a sky dakini
An addictive illusion
Tears welling up in
My eyes. I need
To see her, hold her

In psychological books
I know attachment
Breeds yearning
And then come the pain
I have lost interest

In everything but her
Only her appiration
I cling to which
Brings the pain
And life's suffering

She has a grave illness
So I can't be with her
I suffer along
I would give her
My whole being

My compassion for her
Far exceeds my sexual desire
When, I look into her eyes
This addicts me to her pain

Addiction to love
Is worse than
Addiction to heroin
How do I get detoxed from love?

HEY WHITE MAN

A young man
On the corner
Calls over saying
"Hey white man
What are you
Doingin the "hood"?
Hearing this
Headquarters steps
Out of the car
All 6 foot 3
Of him and
Answers "can
I help you brother?"
The younger one
Steps back replying
"Just saying hello
To the white man"

FOUNDATIONS

In a backyard
On a stone patio
In Westchester,
Three generations,
Eating barbecued chicken;

Walking up stone steps
To a white walled office
In New Jersey,
sitting face to face
Giving counsel;

Alone on a stone floor
Sitting crosslegged
In a Pharping cave,
Make no effort;

Standing by a stone railing,
Face heated
By burning marigolds
And silk draped bodies
Below on the ghat
In Varanasi;
These are the groundings.

Love is grounded
In the held hand;
Compassion is grounded
In the fallen tear;
Joy is grounded
In the leap from the ground,
Wisdom is grounded
In motionless silence.

HEADQUARTERS

I'd phone her
Twice a week
She knew who
Was calling. Never
Picked up my number
Decided to make
A home visit
But she lived
In Newarks Center
Ward. Other clients
Told me don't
Go there. They
Have had drive
By shootings
So I called
A friend.

He was the
main man from
the East Orange
Drug program.
Owned a big
Thunderbird.
Said he'd drop
Me off and wait.
He was about 6
Feet three. Weighed
Over 200 pounds
He drove me
To Newark
As soon as
I step out
Of the car

A young tough looking
Man steps out from behind
A building . "What are you doing
In the hood white man?"
Headquarters, all six foot three of him
Steps out of the car
"Can I help you brother?"
"No sir, just saying hello
To the white man".

HEALING

Full awareness of the emotion
Associated with physical illness
And emotional problems produces healing

Don't treat illness as an
Enemy. Full awarenness
Of the experience is the
Way to heal
Full awareness is
Life as a whole
Without the habits
Of conceptionalization
Judging, evaluating
Labeling
The illness as good or bad

Healing is not
Willing it to be
It is simply permitting
A full awareness
To be present
Each time there is an
Episode associated with
The illness arises.

REFLECTIONS FROM NATIVE POETRY

"O our Mother Earth
O our Father Sky"
Your children are we
With tired backs and tears
We pray to you for gifts
For which we honor you

It is a Garment of Brightness
That all people in every country
Be compassionate to one another
In the white light of mornings
In the red light of evenings
In fringes of falling rain.

In the ceasing of wars
So we can all walk where birds sing
Stroll where grass grows green
Walk the earth with empathy
"O our Mother Earth
O our Father Sky"

Now

Ram Das advises,
"Be here now"
Tolle wrote:
"The Power of Now"
Gangaji teaches,
"Tell the truth,
No stories about
Past or future."
Thich Nhat Hanh
Recommends, "dwell
In the present,
In the present moment
Is the pure land."

Tonight I fall asleep
Suddenly awaken
Got to pee badly
Jump out of bed
Try to make it
I don't, so
I experience
My pajamas as
A soggy, muggy now
This is not
Realm of bliss
It is more
Like a swamp
Tolle and Gangaji
Would council:
"Feel warm and
Soggy,"
No stories or dramas
Be Wet Now.

My Birthday

Birthdays are for people
Who are born howling and wet.
Slapped into the world by a deliverer
Who thinks he's doing you a favor.

You're yanked from the soft home
With the cushiony walls
And built-in pantry
Where you can eat any time you want
And now you're pulled out
And have to wait

Nobody asks you if you want to leave
consults you on a change of address
they just presume its time
and out you come

After you holler and struggle
kick up a fuss
long to get back to the good old days
they up and celebrate your birthday
and say how great it is
that you've been evicted

Nirvana And Samskara

The whole universe is contained
Within each single part
The finite is part of the infinite
The infinite is reflected within the finite
The transcendent is contained with each single part
Nirvana and Samskara are inseparable
Infinity is not held as something out there separate from Samskara
The transcendent is discovered within the nature of Samskara
Infinite truth is found not to be separate from the relative truth
But within it.
Nirvana is to be discovered within the nature of Samskara
Everyone has the potential to become a Buddha
The essence of tantra affirms
The universal Buddha nature right now.

THE BLACK NEWMAN MOMENT

Love is Gustons smeary sky,
Inside is my smothered sigh.
I breathe in then out,
No balm, and no release,
I smother all my grief.

The last great oak
Lost today all its float.
Its leaves scattered on the ground
Night has now crept around.
my tears are kept bound.

I open my mouth
A soundless oath.
Ed Munch's foment,
Silent is its torment,
This black Newman moment

She had poured in my bowl honeyed love
We had talked and eaten for so many years
I lost sight
It was now night,
I covered over my fright

Her long auburn hair
Was no longer there
Her emerald almond eyes
Gone were these ties
She in a field now lies.

Van Gogh's crows come for me
I wait cravenly
Tremble patiently
Knowing love is the bloody smear
Where once was van Gogh's ear

My Guru

I feel a warm glow
In my heart for
My dear, tender Guru
For his wisdom to be
given to me which
Needs to open my heart

The Venerable Ontul Rinpoche
Whom I pray to for the
Removal of all my obstacles.

My Frail Self

I am feeling slightly
Winded these days
I wonder whether
I am out of shape
I feel old and gray as the day

My Doctor examined me
Then asks questions
You sit too much
Eat chocolate all the time
Don't exercise enough

I have no stamina
I can't walk a mile
Never am out in the sun
I don't breathe in
Clean fresh air

I go to the doctors
He recommended exercising
On the tread mill
At least 3 or 4 times
A week on a regular basis

I am to go to the
Doctors special
Gymnasium with many
Exercise equipment
And several treadmills

In a parting comment
He says you look like
A holocaust victim
That just made it
Must build self up

The treadmill and other gadgets all are gray
I stand there, the treadmill gives way and
Like a doomed salmon I struggle hard
Five minutes upstream I'm out of breath

Exercise dominatrix, D cup
Brunhilde demands, "keep your pulse up"
I tell her I'm
Vertically challenged

She never listens "break a sweat"
I say: "At my age I just break wind"
I tell her: "My moisture, like in southwest,
It dries up before it hit's the ground"

Dr Serious shakes his baldhead
"Tests show your bones full of holes."
I try to give spiritual insight
"Doctor, think of me as vast, spacious"

But they know nothing of the spiritual,
So I say my mantra, do treadmill,
Mantra protects mind against doctors,
Treadmills, exams, gray walls and D-cups

THE POLTERGEIST

Do you physicists know about
The energies of the universe?
No you don't. As a Parasychologist
I'm investigating what
A family was telling us was the result
Of a "ghost in the house"

Soy sauce on the ceiling etc.
Ketchup bottles on the walls etc.
The teen aged son who was
Telling us the story suddenly had
His right shoe fly on his foot
Sail across the room, with
Out pitch or yaw, like on a
Conveyor belt and hit the
Wall 8 feet away,
Him not moving a muscle.
I asked my colleague "what was that?
The family answered "its our poltergeist"

So I ask you physicists, energy
Mavins "what the hell was that?"
I was dumbfounded, my colleagues
Were also at a loss to
Explain what happened.
Well you physicists what's your notions?

A Rose Is A Rose Is A Rose

A rose lacks true existence
It is not an object of language or thought
It is beyond the realm of words
Cannot be affirmed or denied
It can not be judged
It arises only dependently
Depending on its seed
The rose arises and is in itself
Nothing inherently independent
A rose is rose is a rose